101

Branding Tips

Practical advice for your brand
that you can use today.

Ed Roach

Compiled from Ed's weekly "Two Cents Worth Branding Tips"
Subscribe at: www.thebrandingexperts.ca/Reluctant/Reluctant.html

Editor: Kim Hutchinson
Book Design: Ed Roach

ISBN-978-098812500-1

For quantity discounts, contact:

Ed Roach, The Branding Experts
268 Seacliff Dr., W. Leamington ON Canada N8H 4E1

ed@thebrandingexperts.ca

To Rosie, the prettiest girl in Leamington.

Well I've done it.

I finally got this book of 101 Branding Tips between two covers. It only took two years, writing a new tip each week to push out to my subscribers to "Ed Roach's Two Cents Worth."

All of the tips offer real opportunities for businesses to improve and grow their brands. Every Wednesday thousands of business people look forward to that week's branding tip. Some are gems and some are meat and potatoes, but all are valuable.

Thank you for purchasing this, my first book. The tips are not industry-specific, and as such are a value for any business person be they owner or employee. Everyone and every business has a brand, whether they want one or not. Keeping that brand in check is the order of the day. 101 Branding Tips is designed to be a quick read and non-intimidating. Branding doesn't have to be complicated.

If you think you've got a quick tip that would be beneficial to the business person, drop me an email and become a Guest Tipster. Email me (Ed Roach) at ed@thebrandingexperts.ca

Have a good read and a chuckle, in some cases.

- Ed Roach

Contents

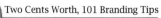

tip1

Where's The Love?

A simple positioning trick is to discover what customers love about you. If you went out of business, what is it that they'd miss?

This little nugget could potentially be what actually differentiates you. Take it, embrace it and sell from it.

tip2

Hold Town Hall Meetings

To help improve communication within your company and develop a culture of clarity, hold regular meetings for all staff including officers.

This step eliminates the rumor mill from being the main source of info.

tip 3

Lucky 13

Every businessperson, at some point in his or her career, has had to prepare an elevator speech. The challenge is to keep it concise while saying what you do. I am president of a networking group, and I insist that our members keep their messages to 13 words or less. This process is not only a great exercise in keeping it relevant, but it helps to keep the meeting moving. An added benefit is the members get a chuckle out of each member's attempt.

tip 4

Culture of Success

Have you just won an award, just
finished a terrific project, expanded
or some other progressive event?
Brag about it to your marketplace.
Clients like to work with
successful influential businesses.

It does wonders for morale.

tip5

3:00 Stretch

This one comes from a peer who found a great way to energize the last few hours in the day. At 3:00 p.m. *every* day, everything stops, music blares and everyones relaxes and enjoys the next 15 minutes to re-charge their batteries and close out the day rejuiced.

tip 6

Walking Managers

Management, including the president should take the time to walk among the employees and interact with them on regular basis.

This personalizes their relationship with you.

tip 7

Who Are You?

Do your employees have any idea
what each of their fellow employees
actually do for the company? Chances
are that they don't. Hold group meetings where individuals tell what they
do for the company. It breeds a better
understanding of how your
company operates.

tip 8

Be An Author

I was reading a discussion on LinkedIn among other professional speakers and it was unanimous: Having your own book increases your expert profile and your ability to gain an audience.

tip⁹

Card Notes

Depending on how you use your card, it's a good idea to consider that someone might want to write a note on them.

For this reason, be sure that there is no varnish or coated surface that resists ink.

tip10

A Simple Brand Awareness Test

Walk up to the first person you see at work and ask them, "What do we do here?" If their answer differs from your preferred answer, then you have a brand problem. It may be time to work on your internal branding. Asking customers and suppliers pits you up against your external branding.

tip11

A Powerful Bit of Wisdom

This was in a client's weekly mailing: "Why is a car's windshield so large and its rear view mirror so small? Because our past is not as important as our future."

So, look ahead and move on!

tip12

A 1-2 Punch For Generating Leads!

On your website, blog or other social sites, you should have a bit of quality FREE content that a visitor can sign up for. On getting this info, they are now part of your lead funnel. From here send them regular quality content where they have additional opportunities to engage your services. It's not enough to just give them information, you have to keep them exposed to your brand, so that when they are ready to act, you are top of mind.

tip 13

Branding Without A Net Is A Risk Worth Embracing

A powerful brand position is one that puts it all on the line and leads. No Plan B means that failure is not an option. You don't need a backup plan.

With branding, you plan for success, you don't plan for failure.

tip14

Plant Some Brand Seeds

Influence a young mind by sharing your wisdom through mentorship programs with a university near you. Where will these young minds be in a few years?

Their influence post-university may lead to lucrative opportunities down the road.

tip15

Online Networking, Offline Results

If you're not networking online, you should be. Recently as part of a few LinkedIn networking groups, I've had the chance to meet members of these groups in offline events. There I've met some interesting opportunities.

Push your brand out there and start building relationships.

tip16

Be The Go-To Person

There is nothing better than helping out someone. Actively try and find resources for people who enter your personal space. Don't try and find an angle for yourself, but help with no strings attached.

Watch your brand soar.

tip17

BAR-B-Q Your Brand

Here's a great idea for the summer company BAR-B-Q. Get a custom branding iron produced and sear that image into your favorite meat or burger on the grill. They can be had at brandingirons.com

tip18

Avoid Shotgun Branding!

Shotgun Branding is marketing multiple services all at once. You usually see this as bullet points. Your best effort would be to take aim with your strongest position that resonates with customers, make your best shot and come home with the prize. The chances of hitting your mark is always better with a concentrated effort rather than a scatter shot to the wind.

tip19

Creating videos for your website

Avoid the urge to add commercials to your website. Rarely do selling videos lead directly to sales. Instead, focus on developing video content that educates your viewers in the form of a tip or demonstration.

This establishes you as an expert or "go to" person on a particular subject.

tip20

Sponsor A Local Adolescent Sports Team

This is not so much to get your logo on a jersey but it is part of giving back to the community. Volunteerism speaks to your brand values. What's more, many of the organizers are also leading members of the business community.

tip21

Domain Email Says Plenty

If you have an email address that ends with something other than your brand name or marketing tagline, you are doing nothing to grow your brand awareness. @gmail, @yahoo, @cogeco "et cetera" makes you look less professional in general. Take every opportunity to push the brand.
This goes for signatures at the bottom of your email as well. When I get email from businesses ending in @gmail, or whatever, I take their intent less seriously.

Sometimes there is a legit reason to do the other. It should be explained, at the very least.

tip22

Change The Conversation

What is the tone and attitude of your brand? Often times businesses takes an "us or them" attitude. This only leads to negative reactions. Change the conversation to how your brand can help your customers with their problems, things that are holding them back. There is no need to bring "them" up at all. Keep the focus on the customer.

The deficiencies of the opponent will become obvious without a word spoken against them.

tip23

Don't Rule Out Print

With online presence and Google rankings taking top priority in business, an area getting little attention is your traditional tools such as postcards and brochures. Done properly these items are still effective in networking situations. With your competition ignoring these old-school media, your use of hardcopy will make you stand out in a great way.

tip24

Clean Sweep The Brand Webs

It's time to clean sweep your brand webs. What has worked? What hasn't? What needs attention? Jot down your top five brand goals and try your best to have them in place during the first quarter. A fresh start is good for all our brands!

I've already begun my top five, starting with a website revamp. I am also adding a mobile version this year.

tip25

Join Networking Groups

Don't just join groups and wait
your turn to say your elevator
speech, but take an active role.
Join committees, offer your
assistance wherever you see an
opening. People are impressed by
go-getters.

tip26

Release Your Inner Author

You are an expert in your field. Take that valuable knowledge and apply it to a subject your potential customers might find compelling. Offer it up on your website or blog for free. Doing this puts you on the path to building a niche group of loyal customers.

tip 27

Free Event - Only $100

Ever wonder how to get people who register for your free events to actually show up? Charge them $100.00 Then offer them a 100% refund when they show up.

How's that for an incentive?

tip 28

Expand Your Personal Brand

If you're interested in strengthening your personal brand, one surefire way is to put yourself out there. Do something that is uncharacteristic of you, or out of your comfort zone. If you're not prone to volunteerism, donate your time to a charitable event. Promote your company through public speaking.

Challenge yourself.

tip29

Great Impression Plan

Always have your best clothes clean
and pressed. You never know when
you might be called upon at short
notice to wear them. For guys,
keep a shaving kit close by as well.

tip30

Email Signature Opportunities

Are you taking advantage of your email signature to push your brand? You can link to your online vehicles, promote special services, and so on.

It's not enough to just put your name anymore.

tip31

Encourage Your Employees To Engage

If you want your employees to be advocates for your brand strategy, do more than spell out rules for engagement. You will be more effective if you get their input as to how they can become part of the delivery.

Tap into their ingenuity.

tip32

Selective Hearing Visionaries: The Best Kind

If you're the sort of visionary who *doesn't* hear "We can't do that!" or "It'll never work," or "Right now's not the time," or "That's beyond our scope," you're just the sort of person whose selective hearing makes you great!

tip33

Learn While They Hold

Take advantage of the time a customer is on hold to introduce them to you brand promise. Record an informative message and push your brand out there using this tried and true LAN line service.

tip34

Idol Worship Is No Idle Thought

You've heard the old adage–
"a picture is worth a thousand
words." With regard to brand
identity this is especially true.
The Nike swoosh, Apple's Apple,
and the Golden Arches are
examples.

Over time people come to identify
with your icon more than the words.
Contemplate an icon for your
business.

tip35

LinkedIn Testimonial

Does this sound familiar? You'd love some testimonials for your LinkedIn profile but feel it's pathetic to ask for one. A solution I use is to go to the profiles of people whose recommendation I'd like, and leave them an unsolicited testimonial. Most times they will reciprocate with a testimonial to you.

tip36

Clear The Dark Clouds

One of the keys to success is positive thinking. Is there someone around you who brings you down? Is there an employee who is a morale killer? Or perhaps it's a client who sucks the life out of you. Do yourself a favor and let these people go. They are better behind you than a barrier in front.

tip37

It Hurts When I Do This

The key to a sale is an interview, and the key to an interview is a disturbing question. Discover the pain point and provide relief.

tip38

Hey pal, can ya gimmie a boost up?

Remember Wimpy from Popeye?–
"I will gladly pay you Tuesday, for a
hamburger today." Give ol' Wimpy
a boost and he will be your
advocate forever. Remember your
childhood friends? When you gave
them a boost over that fence, didn't
they cheerfully share a Coke with
you in the shade later in the day?

Giving a boost to someone is good
for one's soul and great for your
brand.

tip39

Own The Job Site

If your business involves putting teams of people in place, consider branding them with your brand colors. Anyone visiting the job site will become aware of the prevalence of your colors allowing your brand to "own the site" visually.

tip40

Consistency Of Image

Make sure that all your materials have the same brand image. Any deviation only causes confusion among your audience. I go to great lengths to be sure I stay on track with my brand, so should you. Multiple brand images also costs more money to maintain.

tip 41

Instant Blog Audiences

Go on blogs that your audience is on and purposely leave constructive comments. Over time, as you build a reputation, approach the blog owners on, becoming a writer for them. This exposure will lead customers back to you. This is a great way to get the conversation started.

tip 42

Bad Culture = Failed Brand

Your brand environment is made up of a brand perception at the top with an underlying foundation making up the brand culture. Everyone's culture is unique.
Is the day-to-day culture of your organization able to sustain your brand promise? If not it will be short lived. The magic is that they must be aligned to be successful. Your culture makes the brand authentic.

tip 43

Letter Signoffs

How do you sign off your emails and letters? Best wishes, sincerely yours? Why not use your corporate slogan? It reinforces your brand strategy and consistently promotes your company. I sign off with "Lead don't follow."

How about you?

tip 44

Reaching Out

I typically like to try and engage the
audience. If it is a small enough
group (under 20), I get them to tell
us all what they do. This not only
allows them a networking
opportunity but gives me a terrific
feel for WHO my audience is and
how to reach them.

tip 45

Pump Up The Volume

If your brand reflects a company who knows no bounds, then it is your responsibility pump up the volume and take the risks that deliver results. This market is not for the business person who loves to wait and see - that's the mind set of a follower. This is your chance to pump up the volume and make an winning impression.

tip46

Canned BIO

There are many situations (especially online) where it is important to have a good bio and photo of yourself to share. Sometimes it is needed to join social sites. Sometimes a journalist wants more information on you or a prospective customer needs to know more. Keep an updated Bio and photo in a folder and copy and paste wherever you need it.

tip 47

Keyword Cheat Sheet

If you're a prolific blogger like myself, and you have the opportunity to write for different blogs out there, you can submit keywords to help search engines find you and your blog posting. I keep different variations of a list of keywords in a text file that I can submit easily. I do this for keyword links as well.

tip48

Create Your Own Influence

We all have our likes and dislikes when it comes to organized networking groups. Why not organize your own solution and invite kindred spirits into the mix? All the groups have value, but it never hurts to have another arrow in your quiver.

My business relies on referrals, so networking, mentoring and speaking are an essential part of my promotional mix.

tip49

Delivering Your Best

Always deliver your best quality. Sounds like silly advice, but we've all seen the crap some businesses pawn off on people. Even in a rush, poor quality is no excuse and is a bad reflection on your brand. It is very hard to crawl back from. My crowd always states that "You're only as good as your worst effort."

tip50

Face Time Is Important

When distance allows, give your customer as much face time as possible. I can't tell you how many times I delivered a hard copy of a file (rather than emailed it), and walked away with additional projects, just because I was there. One particular day I had three meetings scheduled and all returned additional projects I was unaware of going in.

tip51

Your Time Is The Investment

Even if the person isn't a customer yet, you can really show your class by sending them information you tripped across. I just did this today, to a lead I met at a networking event I attended last night. We were discussing a Deloitte report on emerging media. This afternoon, I located the report online and forwarded it to him. You have to prove that you give a damn.

tip52

From the Horse's Mouth

A surefire way to do a good bit of damage to your brand is to have a weak communication link between management and employees. Due to the times we are living through, any move to streamline a company to be more productive and lean will be the cause for rampant rumors among the employees. A reliable communication plan will halt this dilemma and help reassure staff that all is well. Everyone wants to trust the information at hand, and a communication plan is a great way to start.

tip53

It's Not About You

When developing your marketing materials, don't focus too much on you. Do you really think the prospect cares that much about how big your building is? Stop selling real estate and answer his question – "What's in it for me?" Address his pain and deliver solutions that resonate with him.

tip54

Avoid The Weak Brand

If your brand image doesn't reflect the size and stature of your company, then you need to take a good hard look at your brand image. Does it look like a serious player in your category? Look at your biggest competitors – do they look more successful than you? Chances are they take their image very seriously and didn't just get the cheapest designer to develop it. You can cheap out on carpeting and other hardware, but your brand image is paramount to your success - invest in it wisely.

tip55

Avoiding The Brochure Site

Your website is essentially a print brochure in digital form. If you notice in your visitor stats that visit lengths are incredibly short, then make a large effort to increase the content available on your site.
Be sure that this information is of a quality nature. The more information you provide, the more they will visit to take advantage of it. Another good vehicle for increasing content is a business blog.

tip56

Leverage Your Brand Palette

Every time you promote your small business, the color scheme reflects the immediate message. Develop a brand palette that is used consistently in everything the company helps to sell you. Base the palette on your corporate logo. Over time, your brand palette becomes a recognizable icon in your prospect's mind. Think UPS and brown.

tip57

Get In Their Face

Your sales team needs a follow-up strategy in place. Out of sight - out of mind. Develop a newsletter that goes out to customers AND prospects regularly. Use email marketing to put your name and message in front of their noses. This shows that you care about their success and it will remind them "that you're the person to talk to."

Do it regularly. Forever.

tip58

Give, Give, Give

Go out of your way to find people
you respect for new business leads.
If you join networking groups, join
committees and search out
opportunities for others. In return,
they will actively refer you. You
must give first. Everybody loves
referrals, so developing your own
networking mastermind group can
help promote you with a message of
your choosing.

tip59

Exploit The Niche!

Once you get a healthy number of constituents in your business niche, you can start marketing directly to them based on their common interests. Aim your offers at their unique thirst and build a trusting relationship with them. Develop solutions and content your niches crave. With niche marketing, 100% of your advertising dollars are working for you. With the proper systems in place you can detect exactly who is responding to your efforts to contact them.

tip60

Can They Hear Your Brand?

You don't have to be a multinational to take advantage of sound. Put a few catchy guitar licks at the front end of any presentations you do and marry them with your web presence and you can start to familiarize your audience with a sound icon. With the advent of mobile marketing, a sound icon would be a very powerful introduction. Myself, I'm putting mine to use in a series of podcasts.

tip61

Circle The Wagons. RE-BRAND!

A pretty new image can't cover up a bad brand. Fixing the problem FIRST then delivering on the promise, makes your brand experience compelling. How many of your peers are having slow sales, slow traffic, and so forth and they've decided to "re-brand". They believe that a new logo will solve the issue. They'll see when nothing changes.

tip 62

"Get Them To Ask For It!"

At networking events, engage people in such a way that you entice them to ASK for your card. Just offering it up is more about you than them.

tip 63

Bird Dogs

Familiarize yourself with complimentary businesses who target the same market as your company. Joint promotions allow you to leverage off of each other and maximize budgets.

tip64

Job Prospect For Your Clients

Keep an eye out for opportunities that will benefit your customers. Watch for tools that will be useful to them. Watch your brand value soar!

tip65

Thank You Cards

We are so wired today that simply sending out old-fashioned handwritten thank you cards shows a great deal about your sincerity. Picking up a pen may feel alien, but from those who use this tool, it leaves a strong impression.

tip66

Don't Spill The Popcorn

In our excitement and passion, many a salesperson shows their entire hand to the prospective customer. Telling them more than they need to know could jeopardize your chances for a sale. Only put enough on the table to resonate with their needs. Make sure the best is yet to come.

tip67

Consistency Is Powerful

Let's take a close look at the consistency of your brand image. Does the logo on your business card match the logo on your sign, your website, your stationery, your vehicles and so on? If they differ, then you are sending a confusing message to your audience. If the difference is extreme, they will look as though they represent different companies. If you fail to control your brand image, all other aspects of your brand will be stressed as well.

tip68

YES, Even You Can Enjoy Selling

I heard it said this week, "If you don't enjoy selling, failure is guaranteed." I believe this to be true. Find what fits for you and embrace it. If you enjoy people, networking might be a good fit. If you're more of an extrovert maybe cold-calling is for you. What ever the scenario, find a way to be passionate about sales and let the warmth of success wash over you.

tip69

Slogan Alert!

Take a hard look at your slogan.
Does it echo your positioning
strategy? Does it inspire your
stakeholders? You only have one
chance with potential customers.
Your slogan should sell the
personality and focus of your brand.

tip70

Refine Your Pitch To Reduce Competition

It's understood that for every service or product you take to market you increase your competition times that amount. If you refine your message to one core service or product you limit the number of your competitors. Add one and it doubles, add two it triples and so on.

Choose the one that has the largest return and resonates with customers. A refined brand offering will differentiate and simplify your pitch.

tip71

Bulky-Package Strategy

Bulky-package promotions are three-dimensional materials that are delivered to an intended target to get a meeting with them. While many direct mail materials end up in the trash, sending a bulky-package eliminates this hazard. We've never had one that was not at least opened and viewed.

tip72

Gift Your Services

This is a first for me. I recently had a client give a gift of consulting to a brother of theirs. They bought them, "one hour with Ed Roach."

This wasn't something that I encouraged or even knew about, for that matter. They simply put a check covering the cost of the hour in a card and sent it to them for their birthday. I was humbled to say the least. As an idea, it could be another avenue of promotion for you. Gifting your expertise is a novel way to spread your influence.

tip73

Problems You Can Love!

To help build a lasting relationship with a customer, you first need to listen, discover what problems they are troubled with and take them as your own. Your job is to bring a positive solution to those problems. Your customer will see your value and not forget you.

tip74

Make Your Brand Promise Company-Wide

Your brand promise is the statement that you stake your reputation on. It's what you're delivering to your customers.

Be sure that this promise is understood and delivered by your entire team.

tip75

It's Not About You

Whenever you find or make the opportunity to promote yourself, try to make the message about them. While it is important to brag a little, try to provide solutions to their pain points. It will be easier for your message to resonate with them if they can picture themselves using your solution.

Many ads you see in numerous trade publications go on and on about how great they are and not much about how you can help. So the next time your agency is writing up an ad, put in a little something about "them."

tip76

Make A Difference – Get Noticed

If you're out in the public eye on business, be noticeable. A friendly smile, a distinctive wardrobe or being a helpful connector can go a long way to differentiating your personal brand. Being distinctive pays off in dividends.

It plays into the notion that it's not who you know, but rather who knows you that really counts.

tip77

Jump And Grow Your Wings On The Way Down

The wings referred to in the headline are really the passion and belief in yourself. The only way you are going to succeed is to DO IT. Nike had it right, "Just Do It." If you jump and crash, then your wings were not fully unfurled. But like any new life, you have to grow. You have to brush yourself off and get back up there and jump again.

Each time, you will gain the confidence to learn from past errors and break new ground.

tip78

Pimp Your Attitude

Your employees are inspired or dragged down depending on your attitude. By pimping your attitude, you bring nothing but positive vibes to the company. Even when the economy appears to be spiraling down around you, look for the opportunities and display this to the stakeholders.

A leader who fails to pimp their attitude stands a great chance of losing real talent to the competition.

tip79

Three Strikes - You're Out!

Networking works for me. But I do have a strategy when I take part. After I've decided that the group membership has my customer profile, I dedicate at least three years to making it work. I believe it takes at least this long to build trust, join committees and just get involved. If the group clicks, then of course I continue to contribute and succeed.

Too many people don't even invest six months of their time in networking. These are also the types who look to *get* first instead of *give*.

tip80

The Social Media Spread.

Don't spread your brand too thin on the social media front. Do a few very well and leverage them before adding to your mix or you will not benefit much from any of them.

As more become available, you'll be better able to find a fit with what's working for you.

tip81

Strategic Memberships

Join organizations devoted to your target audience to gain exclusive access to valuable information. Once you have the information you desire, let the membership lapse on the renewal date. Strategic memberships are a form of insider reconnaissance.

tip 82

Taking Notes Shows Respect

Whenever you're in a meeting with a customer, take notes. It not only shows that you take their every word seriously, it shows respect. It's also a way to slow down your intake of information so that you can better comprehend the "nuggets" that emerge.

tip83

The Secret To A Strong Brand

You don't have to be a billion dollar company to be a strong brand. Every day, look for the little things that you can do to make your brand shine. The biggest thing that you can bring to your brand is a friendly smile and a genuine desire to help others succeed.

tip 84

Stop, Talk And Attract

Do you want to improve on your expert profile? Get out there on to the web, look up influential blogs that customers are frequenting and start leaving comments. Join in on conversations and show some value as a leader. Your comments lead readers back to you. On LinkedIn, group discussions are also the place to hang out and comment.

tip 85

Stop Running Your Business!

Are you running your business or leading your business? If you're running it, you've lost your passion for it.

Start leading again and watch the attitudes of the people around you surge.

tip86

This Is A Really Square Tip!

This is an interesting idea to help you stand out at networking events and meeting new prospects - SQUARE BUSINESS CARDS.

Use both sides and create something memorable

tip 87

Whatta ya say?!

Your positioning strategy is your differentiator, which makes you the leader in your category. It should absolutely resonate with your customer.

A slogan on the other hand is an inspirational message that establishes an emotional attachment among all your stakeholders. It is stronger when it compliments your positioning strategy.

Using both is your smartest brand move.

tip88

Video Badges

Here's clever idea. I saw this at a networking event in London, Ontario. I couldn't keep my eyes off of it. It can play actual video and is the size of a business card. It's great for the hospitality industry. It clips to your clothing and the quality is very good. Makes a striking "Hello, my name is" badge.

tip89

Avoid The Follow-The-Leader Brand

If you're not the leader, you're not trying hard enough. Branding wants you to be the leader, and if that's not possible then come up with a new category where you can claim the leadership position. You want to eliminate alternatives. Choice may be good for customers, but it's hell for brands. There is no room for followers here.

tip90

Identify Your Brand Personality

At this point in your brand history,
what would you say is the personality
of your brand? To come to grips with
this question, you're going to have
to picture your brand as a person
walking down the street. How would
you and your stakeholders describe
this person? That description will
give you a good benchmark of how
your personality fares. If the
description is complimentary,
then take pride in that light, but if
it is negative, then take heed and
realize that it is probably costing
you money.

tip91

Why Don't They Like You?

Get a group of stakeholders to describe your brand as a person. If the result isn't someone entirely positive, then maybe that will answer a few questions you may have and deliver starting points for improvement.

tip92

Who Are You?

Do you understand your own brand?
Identify what your brand stands for
and then build on that strength.
If you're seen as an authority on
a subject, then that is your seed
for growth. Your efforts must
strengthen that perception. Don't
be afraid to share your knowledge,
it will come back to you in
opportunities. Sharing also builds
brand advocates.

tip93

You Can't Win If You're Not Playing The Game

Don't hide behind your brand and rely entirely on word of mouth as your sole source of promotion.
A good first step is to send out PR stories to local media and bloggers.

On average, your customer trusts what the press writes. One story can be amazing in generating business. This bit of good news is great for your brand.

tip94

Feel The Pain

You know your brand's gonna suffer when the visionary of the company is dwelling on the downside of the economy. Employees take their lead from management. It's hard to get motivated when the boss wears a noose for a necktie. Discover ways to pump the attitude throughout the company.

tip95

Do You Have A Brand Scent?

Choose a signature odor that you can harness and market. Perhaps is a strong hickory scent for B-B-Q, or a flowery scent for florist, or women's services. Even if you have a motorcycle shop, you could adopt a fresh outdoorsy scent to identify your brand. Cinnabon does a great job with this at mall locations.

tip96

Don't Beg Employees To Take Business From You?

Are you doing your utmost to save a nickel only to create an environment where employees are just waiting for the right opportunity to jump ship? Or worse yet, start their own business and take your best customers with them? Don't do your brand long-term damage by finding ways to shave costs at the expense of those who make you money. Now is the time to invest in equipment and training. Position your brand for growth. Don't add to a culture of fear, but inspire your employees to seek out opportunities by embracing a rejuvenated brand.

tip97

Live Long – Work Like Jackass

I live across from a fruit stand. It is run by an Italian family. When I mentioned that she worked like a dog, the mother, who is 86, said: "I no work like dog. Dogs lazy. I work like jackass!" We had a good laugh. Don't be afraid of hard work. It keeps your body and mind healthy.

It's the only time being a jackass is a good thing.

tip98

Let The World Know You Are An Influencer

Have you ever had an article written about you or your business?
PR plays an important part in building your expert profile.
Letting your constituency know that your opinion matters gives you credibility. It also builds awareness of your brand.

Add this information to your website, resumé and social media profiles.

tip99

A Coffee And A Smile

The core of this tip came from a coaching client in Washington. Essentially what he does is target office buildings, and armed with a coffee and a smile, he introduces himself to front end office staff. He then offers free assistance with any office equipment problems they may be having. He consistently gets new business this way.

tip100

Develop Proof of Value

When a person compliments you it is proof of your expertise. The more people who know of you, the more opportunities you'll have come your way. Get off your butt and meet people. They are out there in networking groups, associations and trade events. Prove your value to them and watch sales improve.

tip
101
whew!

YES! Service Is Great Service.

Sometimes in running your business, policies can get in the way of great service. You should have only one policy and that should be "YES!"

Falling back on a policy is no way to handle a problem.